Stories of GREAT PEOPLE

Sitting Bull's tomahawk

Gerry Bailey and Karen Foster

**Illustrated by Leighton Noyes
and Karen Radford**

Crabtree Publishing Company
www.crabtreebooks.com

Mr. RUMMAGE has a stall piled high with interesting objects—and he has a great story to tell about each and every one of his treasures.

DIGBY PLATT is an antique collector. Every Saturday he picks up a bargain at Mr. Rummage's antique stall and loves listening to the story behind his new 'find'.

HANNAH PLATT is Digby's argumentative, older sister—and she doesn't believe a word that Mr. Rummage says!

COLONEL KARBUNCLE sells military uniforms, medals, flags, swords, helmets, cannon balls—all from the trunk of his old jeep.

Crabtree Publishing Company
www.crabtreebooks.com

Other books in the series
Cleopatra's coin
Columbus's chart
Martin Luther King, Jr.'s microphone
Leonardo's palette
Armstrong's moon rock
The Wright Brothers' glider
Shakespeare's quill
Marco Polo's silk purse
Mother Teresa's alms bowl

Credits
Tom Bean/Corbis: 28 top
Bettmann/Corbis: 9, 10, 15 bottom, 28 bottom, 30 top
Brooklyn Museum of Art/Corbis: 25 center left
Corbis: 22 bottom, 31 bottom
Geoffrey Clements/Corbis: 19 bottom
© Howard Terpning: 16 bottom
Edward S. Curtis/Corbis: front cover
Edward S. Curtis/Library of Congress: 15 top right
Werner Forman/Topfoto: 27 bottom left
Hulton-Deutsch Collection/Corbis: 20 bottom
Leonard de Selva/Corbis: 19 top
Museum of the City of New York/Corbis: 16 top
Roger-Viollet/Topfoto: 21 top, 32 bottom
Stapleton Collection/Corbis: 35 top right
Topfoto: 13 top, 23 top, 26 center right, 27 top right

Picture research: Diana Morris info@picture-research.co.uk

Library and Archives Canada Cataloguing in Publication

Bailey, Gerry
 Sitting Bull's tomahawk / Gerry Bailey and Karen Foster ; illustrated by Leighton Noyes and Karen Radford.

(Stories of great people)
Includes index.
ISBN 978-0-7787-3692-9 (bound).--ISBN 978-0-7787-3714-8 (pbk.)

 1. Sitting Bull, 1834?-1890--Juvenile fiction. 2. Dakota Indians--Kings and rulers--Biography--Juvenile fiction. 3. Hunkpapa Indians--Kings and rulers--Biography--Juvenile fiction. I. Foster, Karen, 1959- II. Noyes, Leighton III. Radford, Karen IV. Title. V. Series.

PZ7.B15Si 2008   j823'.92   C2007-907628-9

Library of Congress Cataloging-in-Publication Data

Bailey, Gerry.
 Sitting Bull's tomahawk / Gerry Bailey and Karen Foster ; illustrated by Leighton Noyes and Karen Radford.
  p. cm. -- (Stories of great people)
 Includes index.
 ISBN-13: 978-0-7787-3692-9 (rlb)
 ISBN-10: 0-7787-3692-X (rlb)
 ISBN-13: 978-0-7787-3714-8 (pb)
 ISBN-10: 0-7787-3714-4 (pb)
 1. Sitting Bull, 1834?-1890--Juvenile literature. 2. Dakota Indians--Kings and rulers--Biography--Juvenile literature. 3. Hunkpapa Indians--Kings and rulers--Biography--Juvenile literature. 4. Little Bighorn, Battle of the, Mont., 1876--Juvenile literature. I. Foster, Karen, 1964- II. Noyes, Leighton, ill. III. Radford, Karen, ill. IV. Title.
 E99.D1S5623 2008
 978.004'9752--dc22
                    2007051262

Crabtree Publishing Company
www.crabtreebooks.com   1-800-387-7650

Published in Canada
Crabtree Publishing
616 Welland Ave.
St. Catharines, Ontario
L2M 5V6

Published in the United States
Crabtree Publishing
PMB16A
350 Fifth Ave., Suite 3308
New York, NY 10118

Published by CRABTREE PUBLISHING COMPANY
Copyright © **2008** Diverta Ltd.

All rights reserved. No part of this publication may be reproduced, stored in a retrieval system or be transmitted in any form or by any means, electronic, mechanical, photocopying, recording, or otherwise, without the prior written permission of Crabtree Publishing Company.

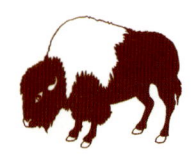

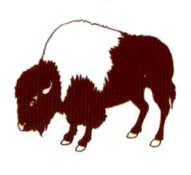

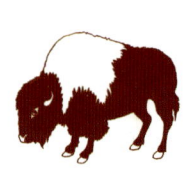

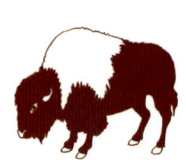

Sitting Bull's Tomahawk

Table of Contents

Knicknack Market comes to life	6
Sitting Bull	9
A young brave	10
Going west	13
Warrior chief	15
The iron horse	16
The gold rush	19
Bluecoat invasion	20
George A. Custer	22
On the run	25
The buffalo spirit	26
Reservations	28
Showman	30
Ghost Dance threat	33
Burial of a chief	35
Sitting Bull's wise words	36
Glossary & Index	37

Every Saturday morning, Knicknack Market comes to life. The street vendors are there almost before the sun is up. And by the time you and I are out of bed, the stalls are built, the boxes are opened, and all the goods are carefully laid out on display.

Objects are piled high. Some are laid out on velvet: precious necklaces and jeweled swords. Others stand upright at the back: large, framed pictures of very important people, lamps made from tasseled satin, and old-fashioned cash registers—the kind that jingle when the drawers are opened.

And then there are things that stay in their boxes all day, waiting for the right customer to come along: war medals laid out in straight lines, stopwatches on leather straps, and utensils in polished silver for all those special occasions.

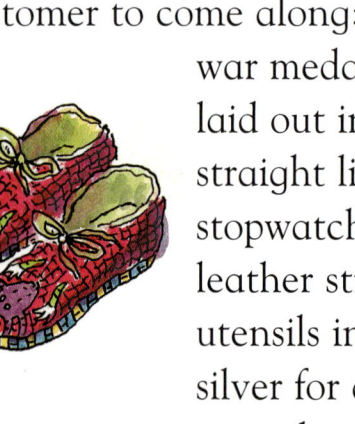

But Mr. Rummage's stall is different. Mr. Rummage of Knicknack Market has a stall piled high with a disorderly jumble of things that no one could ever want. Who'd want to buy a stuffed mouse? Or a broken umbrella? Or a pair of false teeth?

Well, Mr. Rummage has them all. And, as you can imagine, they don't cost a lot!

Rummage's "Antiques"

Digby Platt—ten-year-old collector of antiques—was off to see his friend Mr. Rummage of Knicknack Market. It was Saturday and, as usual, Digby's weekly allowance was burning a hole in his pocket.

But Digby wasn't going to spend it on any old thing. It had to be something rare and interesting for his collection, something from Mr. Rummage's incredible stall. Hannah, his older sister, had come along too. She had secret doubts about the value of Mr. Rummage's goods and felt, for some big-sisterly reason, that she had to stop her brother from buying useless junk.

As Hannah and Digby approached Mr. Rummage's stall, they saw a bright green jeep swing past and park. It was Colonel Karbuncle's jeep. He was a retired military officer who had more war stories than even Mr. Rummage! The Colonel used his jeep to display all kinds of weapons and other army relics gathered from different countries around the world.

"Hey, let's look at what the Colonel's got stashed in the back of his jeep before we visit Mr. Rummage," suggested Digby.

"Just take a peek, Digby, or we'll be here all day," said his sister, impatiently.

"Morning Colonel Karbuncle, got anything new to sell?" asked Digby.

Colonel Karbuncle stood up straight and saluted as he caught sight of the children. "Not new, Digby! Never new! But I do have a lot of old stuff I might just want to get rid of—heh, heh!"

"Wow, look at this!" exclaimed Digby as he pulled an odd stick-shaped weapon out of the back of the jeep. At one end of the stick was a metal ax head, while the other end was shaped like a smoking pipe.

"What on earth is that?" asked Hannah.

"Well," said the Colonel, "you've found a ceremonial **tomahawk**—part ax, part pipe. The great Native American chief, Sitting Bull, used to sit around the campfire and smoke that pipe with other leaders."

"It's beautiful," said Digby, stroking the fine, carved wood. "Can I show it to Mr. Rummage?"

Sitting Bull

The man who came to be known as Sitting Bull, was born in 1831 by the Grand River, which runs through the state of South Dakota. This was an area the Lakota, or Teton Sioux, people called 'Many Caches' after the food storage pits they dug there. Sitting Bull's father was named Four Horns.

Sitting Bull was chief and councilor of the Teton Sioux confederacy. His ambition was to bring together all the Sioux nations. He hoped they could hold on to the remaining lands of the Native people as a sacred inheritance. He called on all the nations to unite against the European settlers who were taking their lands. But in the end he became the last great warrior to **surrender** to the American government.

Let's find out more...

A young brave

When he was very young, Sitting Bull was called 'Hunkeshnee,' or 'Slow,' because he couldn't run very fast. Apparently, his legs were bowed, bent like the ribs of the ponies he loved to ride. He was never seen on foot, but always on horseback.

Sitting Bull

One day, all the boys in the Lakota nations staged a mock hunt with buffalo calves. During the game, Hunkeshnee was thrown by his pony and a large calf angrily attacked him. But the young **brave** wasn't afraid. He grabbed the calf by both ears and struggled with it, pushing it back until the beast was sitting on its backside. "Hunkeshnee has tamed the buffalo calf," the boys cried. "He has made it sit down!" From then on he was known by his familiar name of 'Tatanka Iyotanka,' or 'Sitting Bull.'

Sioux warrior

To be a true leader, Sitting Bull had to prove that he was brave. His first chance came when he led an attack against a war party of the Crow nation. After a battle, the Crows retreated but left one of their chiefs behind. The man was lodged in a deep ditch and he couldn't be allowed to escape. When Sitting Bull raced to the edge of the ditch and struck at the warrior with his spear, it was clear the Crow chief had no bullets left in his gun. He couldn't fight back. So Sitting Bull gave his enemy his own gun, declaring that he wouldn't let a brave man die unarmed. Then he led a second charge. Sitting Bull was badly wounded by his own gun, but his warriors killed the Crow chief.

"Look, Mr. Rummage, look at this!" cried Digby as he ran up to Mr. Rummage's antiques stall.

"That's a fine old tomahawk you've got there," said Mr. Rummage. "Where did that come from?"

"Back of my jeep," said Colonel Karbuncle, "where these two young people found it."

"The Colonel says it belonged to a Native chief called Sitting Bull," said Hannah doubtfully.

"I'm sure it did," said Mr. Rummage. "That looks like a Great Plains ceremonial tomahawk to me, Karbuncle. And, of course, Sitting Bull was from a Plains nation."

"Who lived on the Great Plains?" asked Digby.

"Valiant warriors," explained Colonel Karbuncle, "who rode across the prairies that stretch from the Rocky Mountains to the Great Lakes, and from Mexico up into Canada. I remember the stories my grandfather used to tell. He was there during the wars between Native people and settlers and he often talked about the great nations of the Sioux, the Cheyenne, and the Arapaho. The Sioux were the most powerful, or so he said, and Sitting Bull belonged to a small nation of Sioux called the Hunkpapas."

"They're the Native people who hunted buffalos, aren't they?" said Hannah knowingly.

"That's right," said Mr. Rummage. "For hundreds of years Sitting Bull's nation depended on the meat and hides of the buffalo for their survival. The nation followed the herds as they roamed the plains in search of food."

"I've seen movies of cowboys fighting Native people," said Hannah. "The cowboys always win. Were those the wars you were talking about?"

"Not really," said Colonel Karbuncle, frowning. "Those movies don't tell the real story. No, these battles were terrible and bloody, and didn't show the settlers in a good light."

"You mean they lost?" asked Digby.

Mr. Rummage looked at the colonel, "Oh no, they didn't lose—far from it!"

"What happened then?" asked Hannah.

"Well," began Mr. Rummage, "you have to remember that Native nations lived all over North America before the Europeans arrived. Native people hunted but only took what they needed, and they enjoyed a simple way of life. Without their hunting grounds, the Sioux and the many other nations couldn't survive."

"The settlers didn't see it their way, though," added Colonel Karbuncle.

"The United States was a young country with a lot to learn, and Native people were treated like savages. As settlers moved west, they took Native people's lands by force or by making them sign away their rights."

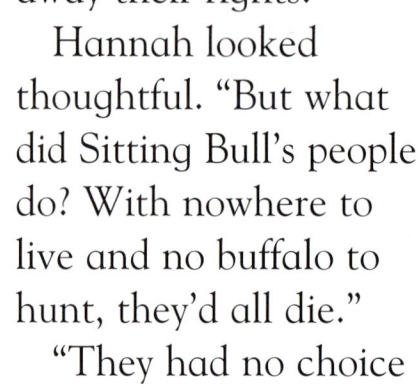

Hannah looked thoughtful. "But what did Sitting Bull's people do? With nowhere to live and no buffalo to hunt, they'd all die."

"They had no choice but to fight for their lives," declared Colonel Karbuncle.

Going West

When the first explorers pushed west towards the Pacific Ocean, they opened the way for many different kinds of people to settle there. The United States was expanding fast. It was the time of fur traders, cowboys, gold **prospectors**, and outlaws. But while they prospered, the Native people paid a heavy price—many nations were being wiped out and their way of life was quickly disappearing.

Broken promises

Some nations tried to fight off the settlers, but they couldn't compete with their weapons and armies. The American government even promised land in return, which was theirs in the first place! And most of these promises were broken—especially when gold was found on Native lands. Army forts were built and wagon trains crossed Native territories, protected by soldiers, or "bluecoats" as the Native people called them.

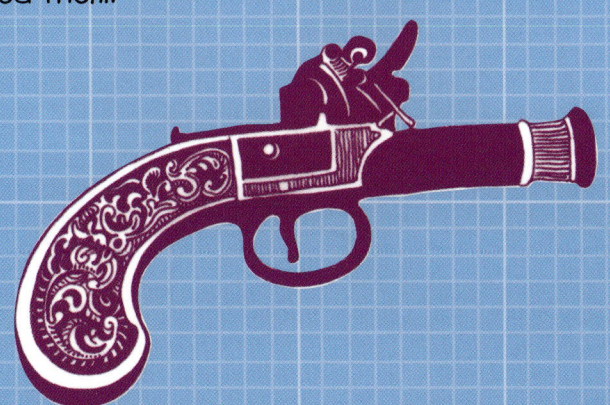

Massacre at Sand Creek

When Black Kettle, chief of the Cheyenne, visited President Lincoln, he was presented with a large American flag. He was told that as long as the flag flew above him no American soldier would fire on him. After making peace in Washington, Black Kettle agreed to stay on a **reservation** at Sand Creek. He thought he was safe. But early on the morning of November 29, 1864, Colonel Chivington and his volunteer militia rode to Sand Creek and killed hundreds of Cheyenne. With so many broken promises, Native people knew they could not trust the bluecoats.

"It must have been hard being a Native leader," said Digby. "I guess you'd have to be really tough and strong."

"You had to be that and more," said Mr. Rummage. "Young warriors would only follow a man who they respected for his courage and actions. And he had to be wise too. The chief was always the spokesman for his people."

"Sitting Bull had all those qualities," added Colonel Karbuncle. "He was brave, a born leader of men, and a wise councilor. Sitting Bull said, 'I am here by the will of the Great Spirit, and by his will I am chief.'"

"But he was also a kind and gentle man," said Rummage.

"Was he married? Did he have kids?" Hannah wanted to know.

"Oh yes. And according to some settlers, he was a good father and husband," said Mr. Rummage. "He had a son called Crow Foot and also a daughter. Although what he'd have made of you two I don't know!"

"He'd have called you 'Little Pack Rat,'" Hannah laughed at her brother.

"And he'd have called you 'Little Big Mouth,'" cried Digby.

"I think he'd have called you both 'Children Without Manners,'" said Mr. Rummage with a grin.

Warrior chief

In 1867, Sitting Bull was named chief of the Teton Sioux nation by his father, Four Horns, who told him, "It is your duty to see that the nation is fed, that we have plenty. When you say 'fight,' we shall fight; when you say 'make peace' we shall make peace." Four Horns gave Sitting Bull a war headdress of black and white eagle feathers. Each feather stood for a brave deed carried out by the best warriors in the tribe.

Fort Laramie Treaty

In 1851, when the Plains nations signed the Fort Laramie **Treaty**, they believed they weren't giving up their lands. They just agreed to let the government build a few roads and forts. However, ten years later, they had built far more than that, and now they wanted more land and another treaty. Some chiefs agreed. Others, including Sitting Bull, didn't. Some of the younger Native people were angry and raided settlers' camps and attacked forts. It was going to be war or starvation. Sitting Bull said, "My brothers, shall we submit? Or shall we say to them, 'First kill me, before you can take possession of my fatherland.'"

The iron horse

The clanging of rails being laid, and the whistle and smoke of the steam engine must have shattered the peace of the Great Plains. Settlers saw the railroad as progress. Native people saw it as a threat because it brought even more explorers and adventurers to the west. Unfortunately, the railroads created change that no one could control. The "iron horse" became a symbol of the clash between two very different ways of life.

Singing rails

In 1868, the Northern Pacific Railroad broke the Treaty of Laramie by laying tracks over Native lands. When railroad workers began to survey the Yellowstone River Valley, the Sioux attacked them. Other nations, including the Cheyenne and Arapaho, also tried to defend their land by sending out war parties and tearing up the tracks. They put their ears to the tracks and listened to the "singing" of the rails, so they could tell when a train was coming and lay an ambush for it.

The Battle of Yellowstone

The Battle of the Yellowstone River, where soldiers were protecting railroad workers, was another fight in which Sitting Bull showed his true courage. Cooly, he led four other warriors out to a spot between the rails. There, they sat down and calmly shared a peace pipe as bullets screamed all around. When they had finished, Sitting Bull cleaned his pipe and the five warriors rose to their feet and casually walked away.

"Sitting Bull didn't like the settlers' way of life, and he didn't want his people picking up their bad habits, like drinking whiskey," said Mr. Rummage. "Nor did he like the arrival of roads and telegraph poles."

"And don't forget that blot on the landscape, the 'iron horse,'" added Colonel Karbuncle.

"Iron horse!" exclaimed Digby. "What's that?"

"It's a steam train. The Native people called it an iron horse because it huffed and puffed like a horse that was made of iron."

"Can you imagine what Sitting Bull's people thought when they first saw a train," said Hannah. "They must have been terrified."

"And it changed the face of America, too," Mr. Rummage went on. "It brought more and more settlers to the west and also destroyed herds of buffalo."

"You mean the trains ran over them?" interrupted Digby.

"I expect they did sometimes. But many buffalo were also killed to provide food for hundreds of railway workers, and they were even hunted for sport. Imagine, people shot at them from the windows of trains as they puffed across the plains. It was destructive, selfish behavior."

"Why didn't the settlers just stay on their own land if they didn't want to get killed by Sioux warriors?" said Hannah. "And couldn't they have built roads around the Native territories instead of crossing them? Sounds like common sense to me."

"Well," began Colonel Karbuncle, "settlers were only part of the problem. Things got really bad when prospectors heard that there was 'gold in them thar hills.' Greed my young friends, greed…"

"Yes," said Mr. Rummage, "and the hills in question, just in case you were wondering, were the Black Hills of Dakota. But they weren't just any hills with gold underneath. They were special."

"How were they special? Were they haunted?" asked Digby.

"Well, sort of," said the Colonel. "There were ghosts in them."

"Wow! Real ghosts?"

"What the Colonel really means," Mr. Rummage went on, "is that the hills were sacred to the Plains nations because they thought they stood at the center of the world made by the Great Spirit."

KEEP OUT!

The gold rush

In 1874, Lieutenant Colonel Custer led a band of soldiers into the Black Hills of Dakota. When he returned, he reported that he had found gold there. This led to the government trying to buy the land. But the Black Hills were sacred to the Sioux and they refused to sell. This didn't stop the gold hunters, though. The idea of gold created great excitement among settlers and it wasn't long before a full-scale **gold rush** was on.

Mining towns

People came from California, Australia, Brazil, and England to try their luck. In 1876, the now famous city of Deadwood was built in the area for miners and other newcomers. Villages were built around the mines. Prospectors and adventurers lived lawless lives, stealing from, attacking, and killing Native people.

Meeting at White River

In 1875, a group of American officials met with some of the chiefs of the Sioux and other nations at a place called White River. They thought they'd be able to strike an easy deal to take possession of the Black Hills. But they were in for a shock. Sitting Bull and the other leaders listened, but they wouldn't give in. The officials were forced to pack up and return to Washington empty-handed. Shortly after, all Plains nations were told to move to government-protected lands called reservations. But Sitting Bull stood his ground. This was really a declaration of war!

"I bet Sitting Bull was really angry now," said Digby. "All those miners taking over their sacred lands."

"Yes," said Mr. Rummage, "he had to do something—fast. So he called a meeting of his nation and led them in the Sun Dance, a ceremony performed each year when prayers are offered to Wakan Tanka, the Great Spirit. That's where he told them about his vision."

"What was that?" asked Hannah. "Sounds like a weird sort of dream."

"It was," continued Mr. Rummage. "The Sioux often went without food so they became faint with hunger and had visions, often about battles. Apparently, Sitting Bull's vision showed soldiers dropping into their camp, like grasshoppers falling from the sky…"

Bluecoat invasion

Not many Native people obeyed the government's order to live on reservations. In March 1876, General Crook's bluecoats attacked a group of Cheyenne and Sioux camped near the Little Powder River. They burned tepees, stole ponies, and destroyed food. Most of the Native people escaped, but later that night they crept to where the soldiers were camped and stole back their horses. Then they disappeared into the hills and made their way to Crazy Horse's Sioux village where they were made welcome. The Sioux chief prepared his men for battle.

Battle of the Rosebud

When Cheyenne scouts spotted a column of bluecoats camped in the valley of the Rosebud River, they knew that General Crook was coming for them. The Native people had to strike, so Sitting Bull, Crazy Horse, and Two Moon led a war party of one thousand Sioux and Cheyenne towards the soldiers' camp. Crazy Horse shone in battle. He had studied the way the bluecoats fought and knew he could defeat them. When Crook ordered his men to charge, Crazy Horse used his knowledge to confuse and divide the bluecoat ranks, and eventually won the battle. The next morning, Cheyenne scouts confirmed that Crook's men had retreated south. Sitting Bull's vision of the bluecoat defeat had turned out to be true.

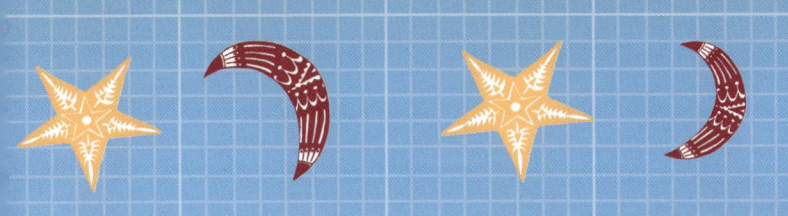

Sitting Bull's Sun Dance

As the weather got warmer, the Sioux, the Cheyenne, the Arapaho, and others joined Sitting Bull at his camp by the Rosebud River to celebrate the annual Sun Dance. Sitting Bull danced for three days, slashed his arms with a knife, and gazed at the sun until he fell into a trance. When he awoke he told his men about a strange vision he'd had. He'd seen bluecoat soldiers falling like grasshoppers from the sky, their heads down and their hats falling off, dropping right into the Sioux camp!

"Did Sitting Bull's warriors chase after the soldiers and kill them all?" asked Hannah.

"Oh no," said Colonel Karbuncle. "While the bluecoats ran away, Chief Sitting Bull led the Sioux to a new camp on the Little Big Horn River. Now there's a name to remember—Little Big Horn…"

"Anyway," he continued, "Sitting Bull's people were joined there by more nations who'd moved off the reservations to follow him—10,000 warriors in all. Of course, he didn't know that Lieutenant Colonel George A. Custer and his 7th Cavalry were heading his way. 'Long Hair' Custer was about to make his last stand…"

George A. Custer

George Armstrong Custer was a dashing army officer with flowing hair and a drooping mustache. He made a name for himself during the Civil War and was known to be a hot-headed young officer. In November 1867, he led his troop of bluecoats into Chief Black Kettle's peaceful camp on the Wichita River. The raid began at dawn and took the Native people by surprise. Around 100 people were killed and 50 women and children captured. Custer ordered all 800 ponies to be slaughtered and the camp burned. It was a **massacre** as terrible as Sand Creek four years before.

Custer's last stand

Custer's success didn't continue. His famous attack on Sitting Bull's huge camp was his last. He ordered some of his men to cross the river and attack from the south, where Hunkpapa and Blackfoot lodges stood. But when Native sentries gave the alarm, Oglala and Minneconjou warriors leapt on their ponies and raced to help. As Custer's men began firing, bullets ripped through tepees. But then the Cheyenne joined in and soon the Native warriors began to push the soldiers back in a cloud of dust, smoke, and confusion. Meanwhile, the rest of Custer's men approached from behind a hill. They didn't see the hundreds of warriors hiding in a ravine. When they got close enough, the warriors charged "like bees out of a hive." The 7th Cavalry didn't stand a chance. All of them were killed, including Custer.

"What happened to Sitting Bull?" asked Digby. "Did he survive the battle?"

"He did," said Mr. Rummage. "But the government was furious. It thought the Native people should be punished for killing Custer and his cavalry."

"But it was the bluecoats who charged first," said Hannah.

Mr. Rummage nodded. "Even so, it wasn't long before troops were swarming over the area and pursuing the Native nations. Sitting Bull and his Hunkpapas fled over the Big Horn Mountains and across the border into Canada, where they thought they'd be safe."

"So he won the battle but he lost his home," said Digby sadly.

"Yes," said Colonel Karbuncle, "it was not really fair. But the government decided to offer him a pardon if he came back and lived peacefully on a reservation. He turned them down several times."

"I suppose he knew that they didn't keep their promises," said Hannah.

"That's right, and it was a very sad day when he was finally forced to surrender. It was his son, Crow Foot, who handed over Sitting Bull's gun and a tomahawk pipe—possibly the very one you're holding, young Digby.

The great chief promised he'd teach the boy to be "a friend to the Americans." He also wanted to be remembered as the last Sioux to surrender to the American government."

"And so he was," added the Colonel gloomily, "so he was."

On the run

With bluecoats hot on his tail, Sitting Bull and his Hunkpapas fled to the north. Meanwhile, the government took control of all reservations in Sioux territories and treated the people there as prisoners of war. The chiefs were forced to sign legal documents handing over the Black Hills and the Powder River. Yet another treaty had been pushed aside.

A new home

Sitting Bull refused to give in to the government. But this meant he had to find safety in nearby Canada. In May 1877, he and his battle-weary Hunkpapas crossed the Canadian border, determined to settle there. Sitting Bull was told he could stay as long as he and his people obeyed the law.

Starvation

But the Canadian government didn't really want Sitting Bull in the country. They thought he'd make trouble sooner or later. So the Hunkpapas weren't given food or clothing. And when winter set in, they starved in the bitter cold. At one point, Sitting Bull heard that Father Huggonard of the Lebret Mission in the Qu'Appelle Valley had ordered a shipment of flour. Sitting Bull was so desperate to trade with him that he offered Huggonard a beautiful Navajo blanket, saying "How much will this buy?" But his efforts were in vain. There were hardly any buffalo left to hunt on the plains, and Sitting Bull had to save his people.

Sitting Bull surrenders

In 1881, worn out by worry and hardship, Sitting Bull finally gave in and agreed to go to Fort Buford in Montana to surrender. With a heavy heart, he gave up his freedom and agreed to stay on a reservation.

The buffalo spirit

The Plains nations respected the earth and honored the buffalo. They believed that the buffalo, or "tatanka," was created by the Great Spirit and had the same right to the land as they did. They believed the spirit of the buffalo helped them to have many children and healed the sick. Their most honored animal was the white buffalo—a rare albino they believed was the sacred leader of the herds.

Buffalo ceremonies

The buffalo gave life to the Plains nations and different groups performed ceremonies to call the herds. They used sacred buffalo skulls, buffalo-shaped stones, and even hairballs from the buffalo's stomach to celebrate these rituals. The hunters always thanked the spirits for a kill.

Following the herd

For hundreds of years the buffalo herds roamed the great, grassy plains of Canada and the United States. They were once so numerous that they stretched as far as the eye could see. Native people called them "thunder of the plains" because their stampede across the plains sounded like the roll of distant thunder.

When Europeans came

Europeans changed the way Native people hunted buffalo. Instead of hunting on foot, they rode on swift ponies and used deadly rifles to shoot the buffalo. For settlers, buffalo hunting meant the danger and adventure of the "wild" west. The government actively encouraged buffalo hunting as a way of keeping so-called "hostile" Native people under control. They hired professional hunters to kill the animals. Soon there were hardly any buffalo left on the plains.

Buffalo arts and crafts

Native people used every bit of the buffalo—nothing was wasted. They used the hides to make tepees, clothes, saddles, and shields. Meat was dried and eaten all year round, and fat was used for lamps. Buffalo hair was used to make rope, blood was used to make war paint, and horns and bones were carved to make tools. Ribs made good sleds and snowshoes for the winter, the stomach was used to make cooking pots, and dung fueled the campfire.

Reservations

In exchange for taking Native land, government reservations were given to the people to live on for as long as they wanted to. The nations were also granted a supply of food and other things they needed—as long as they stayed on the reservations. In the beginning Native people were allowed to leave their reservations to hunt buffalo, but that soon changed, and anyone caught off a reservation was considered hostile and could be shot. The system was unjust and meant Native people lost their freedom and dignity, and sometimes also their will to live.

Missionaries and government agents wanted to wipe out Native culture, so many children were separated from their parents and made to attend special schools. It was hoped they wouldn't be influenced by the "old ways" of their people.

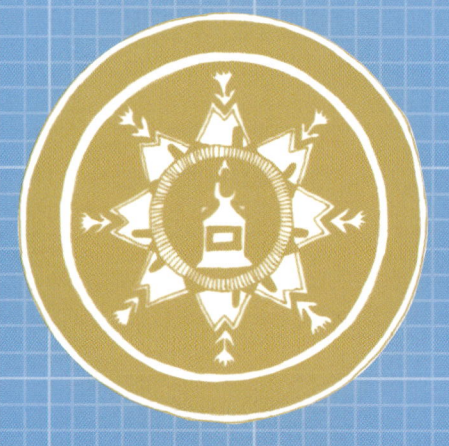

Standing Rock Reservation badge

Native children were made to wear school uniforms.

"Why did Native people hate living on reservations so much?" asked Digby.

"It meant loss of freedom," said Colonel Karbuncle. "And no one likes to lose their freedom. They were used to roaming the plains, hunting for buffalo. And they wanted to keep on doing it."

"Not only that, but the reservations got smaller and smaller," added Mr. Rummage. "Some nations ended up with plots of useless land they couldn't hunt on. So they were forced to depend on handouts from the government. It was a sad end to their way of life."

"And even Sitting Bull had to come back to a reservation in the end," said Hannah.

"Yes," said Mr. Rummage, "although he asked to be sent back to the Little Missouri River near the Black Hills. But the government wanted him where they could keep an eye on him, so they sent him to the Standing Rock Reservation in South Dakota. Later they moved him further down the river to Fort Randall. He and his Hunkpapas were held there as prisoners of war for two years."

"That's terrible," cried Hannah, "the government should've been ashamed of themselves."

"Later, many people were. But before that happened, living conditions got steadily worse. Sitting Bull was eventually freed—but he was forced to work in the fields, which was no place for a proud Sioux, let alone one of their greatest chiefs."

"Didn't Sitting Bull join Buffalo Bill's Wild West Show?" asked Hannah.

"He did, indeed," replied Mr. Rummage. "In fact, he was the star attraction."

"Wow! I bet he liked that. I know I would," said Digby enthusiastically.

"Come on," scowled Hannah, "he was a great leader. Can you imagine a king acting in a play about the royal family? He must have hated it."

"You may be right, Hannah," said Colonel Karbuncle. "He was paid $50 for riding once around the arena. Then he got tips for signing his autograph. It was mighty undignified if you ask me. He agreed to do one season but then he said his people needed him at home."

"He'd been shocked by the different way of life, you see," added Mr. Rummage. Especially the poverty and neglect he saw in the cities. He once said to sharpshooting Annie Oakley, the famous cowgirl, 'The white man knows how to make everything, but he doesn't know how to share it.'"

Showman

Buffalo Bill Cody's show featured sharpshooting, racing, and rodeo-style events. Sitting Bull put on his war headdress and warrior's clothes and starred in recreations of battles he'd actually fought in, like Custer's Last Stand—except that, this time, Buffalo Bill would ride in and save the day. Most Native people who joined up with Buffalo Bill did so to escape life on the reservations and to earn money. Sitting Bull, however, gave most of his earnings away. Cody exaggerated the lifestyles of Native people to make his show more dramatic. Despite this, he is said to have always treated the Native people with great respect. Apparently, Sitting Bull called him his friend, and there are a lot of photographs of them standing together.

By Grand River

When Sitting Bull returned from the show, he lived in a cabin on the Grand River, near his birth place. He still refused to live by the government's rules, although he did agree to send his sons to school. He believed the next generation of Sioux should be able to read and write. But he advised his people to take from American culture only those things that were useful and to leave the rest alone.

Land grab

In 1888, the government wanted more land for settlement. It decided to carve up the Great Sioux reservation into six smaller reservations. Sitting Bull tried to persuade the Native leaders that they were being swindled. It worked and the commissioners had to return to Washington empty-handed. But after more threats, the land was eventually sold and Sitting Bull's reservation was broken up.

Sitting Bull starred in Wild West shows.

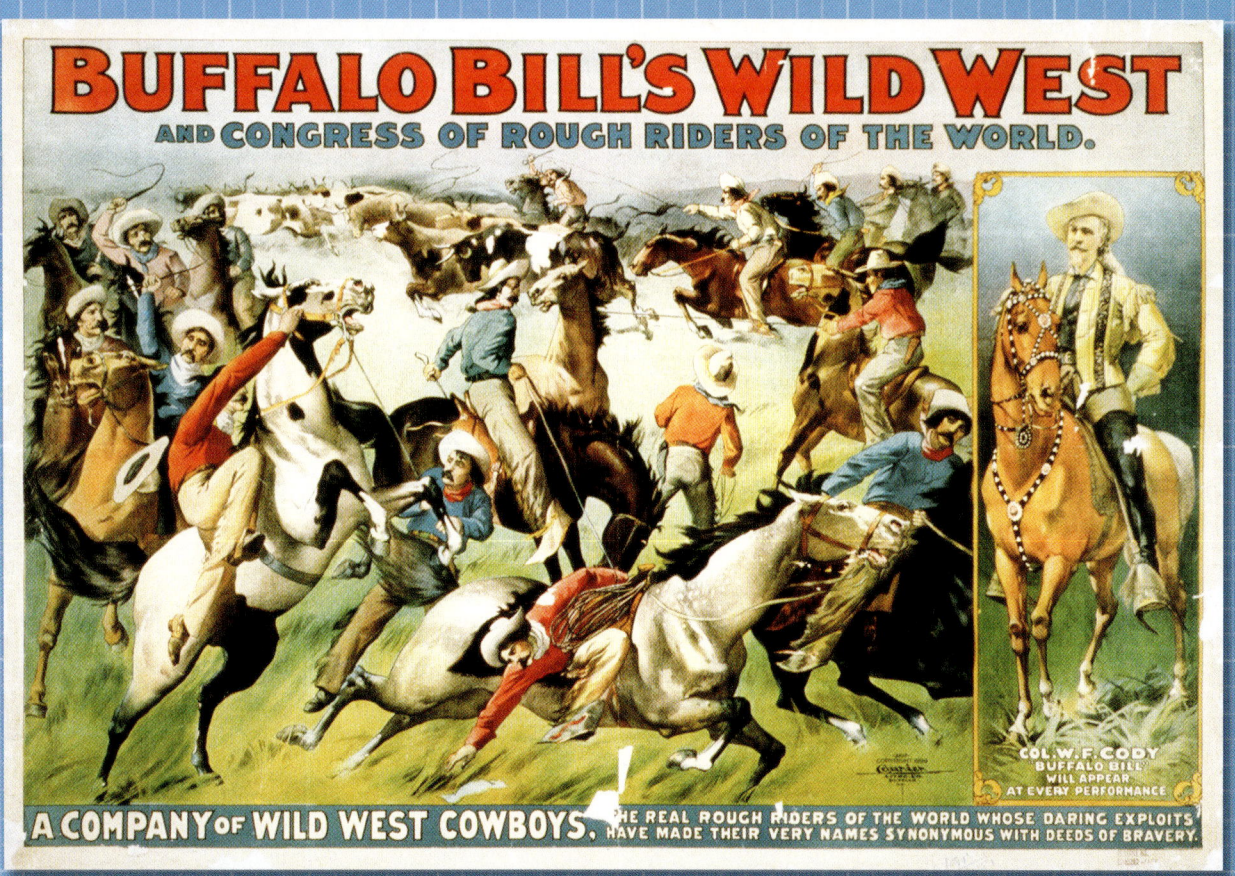

"Was that the end of Sitting Bull?" asked Digby.

"Not quite," replied Mr. Rummage. "About a year after the breakup, a Sioux called Kicking Bear came to talk to Sitting Bull. He told him about a wise leader called Wovoka who taught a dance called the Ghost Dance."

"What's a Ghost Dance—is it spooky?" asked Digby.

"Kicking Bear said it was a religious ceremony," replied Mr. Rummage. "Apparently, Wovoka told his followers to dance in circles, until he said it was enough. Then he'd tell them what it meant."

"Sounds weird to me," said Hannah.

"Well, the government thought it sounded dangerous and that the Ghost Dance was really a kind of war dance," continued Mr. Rummage. "After all, Wovoka did say that one day, fresh grass would grow on the plains bringing great herds of buffalo and that the warriors who'd been killed in battle would rise up and join the living. He also foretold that they would have their land back and that the settlers would disappear."

"Who'd believe all that, though?" said Hannah.

"Many Plains nations did. To them it meant hope after losing their freedom and way of life," said Mr. Rummage.

"But it sure scared the government. Especially when they found out Sitting Bull was involved," added the colonel. "Didn't do him much good, though. Stories tell how the old chief had one last vision—something to do with a lark's song. A few years before, he'd dreamt a meadowlark had told him, 'Your own people will kill you.' And it turned out the darned bird was right."

Ghost Dance threat

The authorities were afraid that the Ghost Dance might spark a new Native uprising. They didn't realize that Wovoka had said that no violence was to be used to make change—that the Ghost Dance was enough. Once they heard that Sitting Bull was involved, they decided to send Native police to arrest him. On December 15, 1890, 43 police officers surrounded Sitting Bull's cabin. Lieutenant Bull Head went in and asked the chief to accompany him. When Sitting Bull walked outside, a crowd of Ghost Dancers had gathered. A voice shouted not to go and so he hesitated. Then the police began forcing him to his horse. A gunshot sounded, then another. Sitting Bull was shot through the head and killed by the police. The meadowlark's "prophecy" had come true.

Who was to blame?

Some newspapers reported that Sitting Bull had been killed because he knew the government and Native agents had been making secret deals about how Native people should be treated. In any event, his killing by Native police allowed the government to claim that the Native people themselves were responsible.

Wounded Knee

The final defeat of the Sioux people took place at Wounded Knee Creek. On December 28, 1899, about 300 Sioux men, women, and children were massacred at the hands of American soldiers.

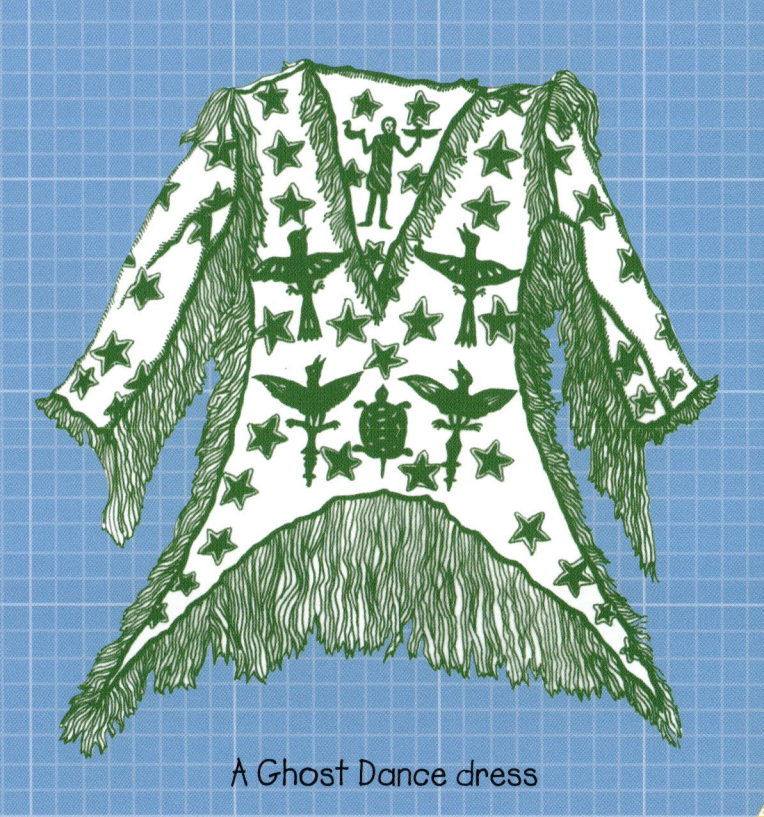

A Ghost Dance dress

"That's really sad," said Hannah. "Sitting Bull's poor people left without a home, and their way of life gone forever."

"It was a terrible tragedy," agreed Mr. Rummage. "In just a few years, the Sioux nations, along with a whole lot of other Native people, were almost destroyed."

"And they'd have all disappeared if some of those bluecoats had had their way," barked Colonel Karbuncle.

"But there are still some Native nations left, aren't there?" said Digby.

"Oh yes. It took time, but Native people gradually organized themselves into true nations once again. The Sioux are a good example," said Mr. Rummage.

"And don't forget the Iroquois—they're still here," added the Colonel. "In fact, many nations are winning back land that was taken from them illegally."

"I can't wait to show everyone my tomahawk and tell them all about Sitting Bull," said Digby.

"Come on 'Sitting Antique Hunter,'" said Hannah leading Digby away. "If we don't get home for lunch, someone's going to get into trouble—and it won't be me…"

Burial of a chief

Sitting Bull was buried without tribal songs or ceremonies at Fort Yates in North Dakota. But he is remembered today as a great and inspirational leader as well as a brave warrior. He never gave in to the demands of the American soldiers and learned not to trust the government's promises. He was revered as the chief-of-chiefs among the Sioux and led his people, the Hunkpapas, with as much care and consideration as he could. Only their hunger and poverty drove him to surrender to the American military—the last Sioux warrior to do so.

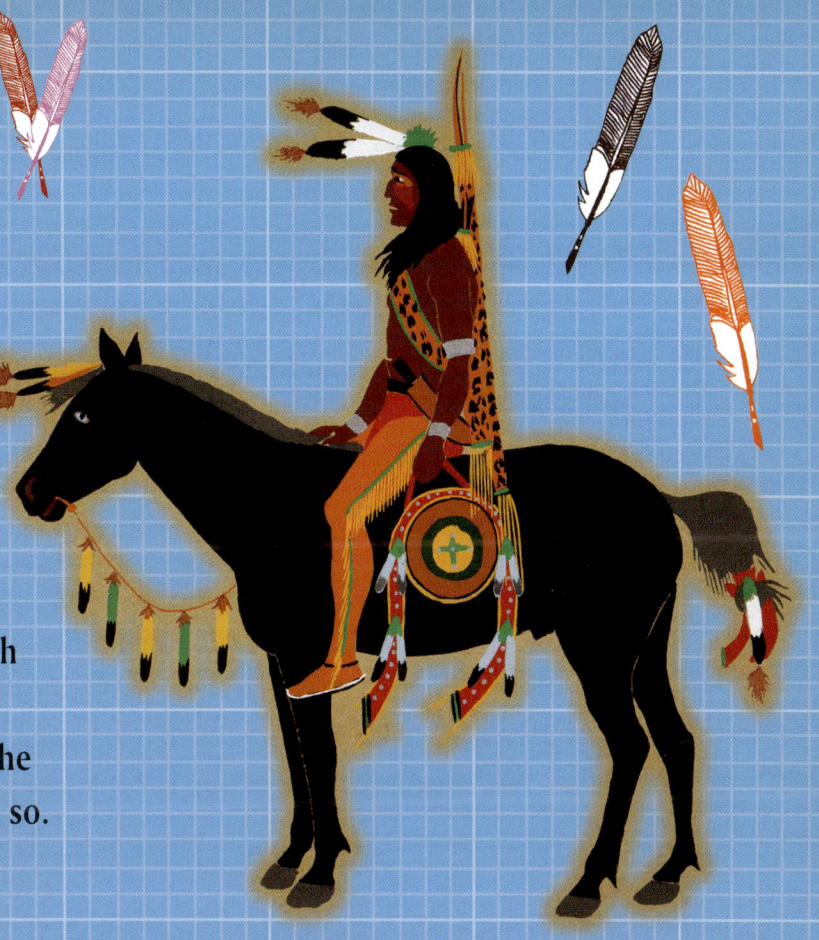

Sitting Bull speaks:

"When I was a boy, the Sioux owned the world. The sun rose and set on their land. They sent 10,000 men to battle. Where are these warriors today? Who slew them? Where are our lands? Who owns them?"

Sitting Bull's wise words

During his life, Sitting Bull's wisdom shone through in many of the things he said. Here are a few of the great chief's best known sayings:

"If the Great Spirit had desired me to be a white man he would have made me so in the first place. He put in your (non-Native) heart certain wishes and plans, and in my heart he put other and different desires. It is not necessary for eagles to be crows."

"I am here by the will of the Great Spirit, and by his will I am chief."

"In my early days, I was eager to learn and do things, and therefore I learned quickly."

"Each man is good in the sight of the Great Spirit."

"Now that we are poor, we are free. No white man controls our footsteps. If we must die, we die defending our rights."

"What white man has ever seen me drunk? Who has ever come to me and left me unfed? Who has seen me beat my wives or abuse my children? What law have I broken?"

"Is it wrong for me to love my own? Is it wicked of me because my skin is red, because I am a Sioux, because I was born where my father lived, because I would die for my people and my country? God made me an Indian."

Glossary

brave A Native American warrior
gold rush A rush of people from many countries to an area where gold has been discovered
massacre The killing of a large number of men, women, and children
prospector A person who looks for gold
reservation An area of land set apart by the federal government for a special purpose, especially one for the use of a Native American people

surrender To give up or give back something that has been given
tomahawk A light ax used as a tool or weapon by certain Native American peoples
treaty A formal agreement between two groups of people

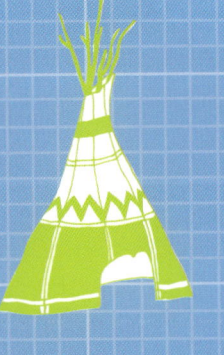

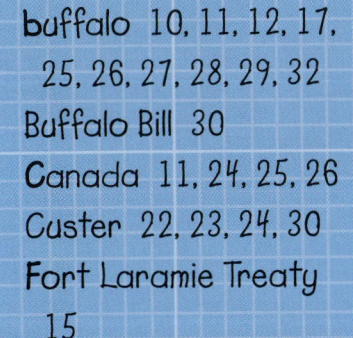

Index

buffalo 10, 11, 12, 17, 25, 26, 27, 28, 29, 32
Buffalo Bill 30
Canada 11, 24, 25, 26
Custer 22, 23, 24, 30
Fort Laramie Treaty 15

Ghost Dance 32, 33
gold rush 19
massacre at Sand Creek 13
Plains nations 11, 15, 18, 19, 26, 32
railroad 16, 17

reservation 13, 19, 20, 22, 24, 25, 28, 29, 30, 31
Sioux 9, 11, 12, 15, 16, 18, 19, 20, 21, 22, 24, 25, 29, 31, 32, 33, 34, 35, 36
Sun Dance 20, 21
Wounded Knee 33

Other characters in the Stories of Great People series.

Mr. POLLOCK's toy stall is filled with string puppets, rocking horses, model planes, wooden animals—and he makes them all himself!

PRU is a dreamer and Hannah's best friend. She likes to visit the market with Digby and Hannah, especially when makeup and dressing up is involved.

KENZO the barber has a wig or hairpiece for every occasion, and is always happy to put his scissors to use!

BUZZ is a street vendor with all the gossip. He sells treats from a tray that's strapped around his neck.

SAFFRON sells pots and pans, herbs, spices, oils, soaps, and dyes from her spice kitchen stall.

Mrs. BILGE pushes her dustcart around the market, picking up litter. Trouble is, she's always throwing away the objects on Mr. Rummage's stall.

Mr. CLUMPMUGGER has an amazing collection of ancient maps, dusty books, and old newspapers in his rare prints stall.

JAKE is Digby's friend. He's got a lively imagination and is always up to mischief.

CHRISSY's vintage clothing stall has all the costumes Digby and Hannah need to act out the characters in Mr. Rummage's stories.

PIXIE the market's fortuneteller sells incense, lotions and potions, candles, mandalas, and crystals inside her exotic stall.

YOUSSEF has traveled to many places around the world. He carries a bag full of souvenirs from his exciting journeys.

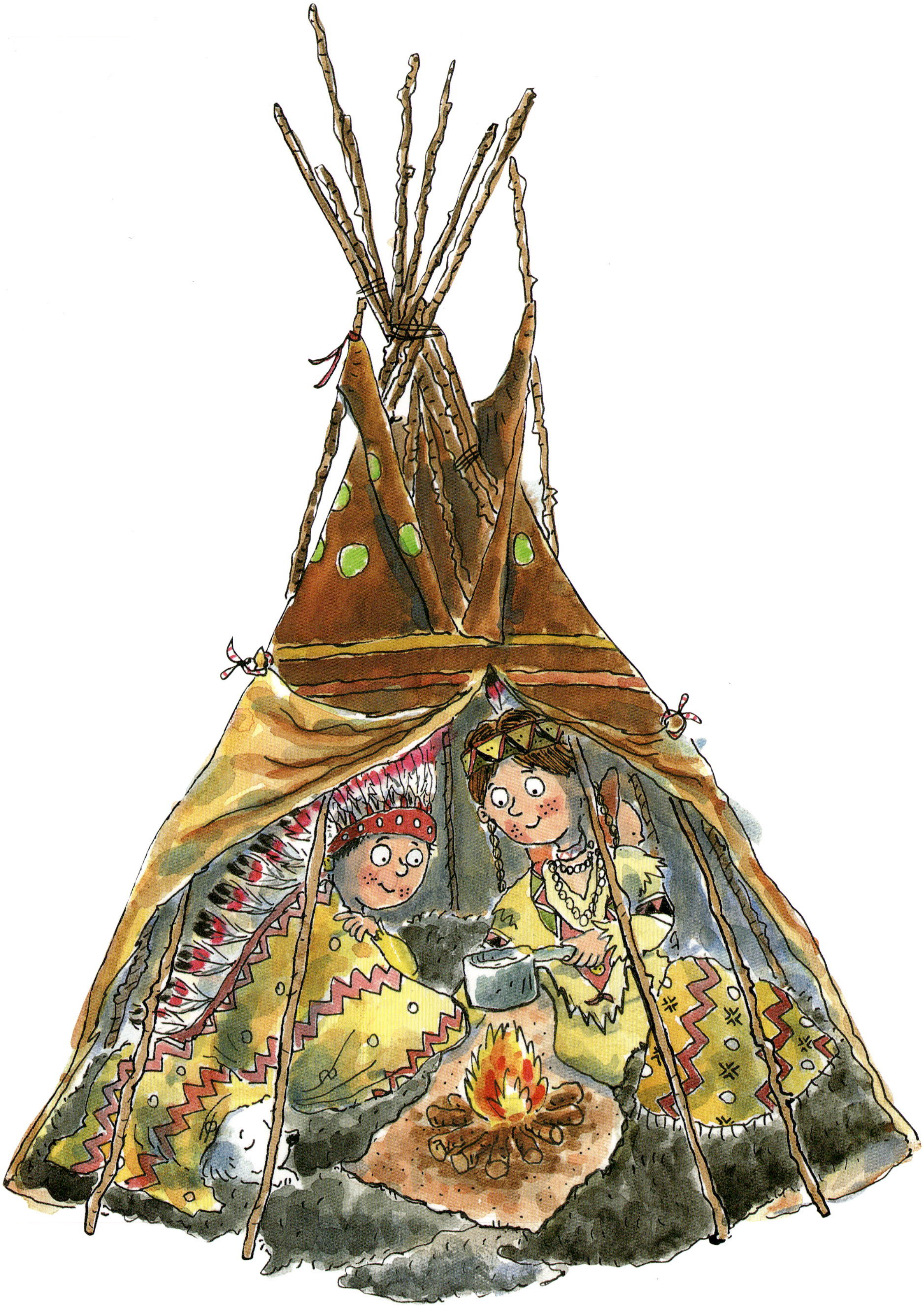